prolog

The application consists of a written and an oral part (interview).

In this e-book, the cover letter is treated exclusively.

The cover letter is the central ticket to get into the selection.

Brevity and conciseness distinguish a successful cover letter.

The four parts of the witten application are:

The welcome formulation.

Professional qualifications

Personal qualifications.

Final sentence.

All other versions are generally unnecessary and reduce your chances of being invited.

The tabular form of the CV is the most successful. There are only two good variants. The shape with annual figures and the monthly data.

The written application

The four parts of your letter are:

Welcome formulation.

Professional qualifications.

Personal qualifications.

Final sentence.

The cover letter is the central ticket to get into the selection.

Short and conciseness distinguish a successful cover letter.

The cover letter usually involves four parts! There are exceptions.

Not more!!!!!!!!

The four parts are:

Welcome formulation.

Professional qualifications.

Personal qualifications.

Final sentence.

Examples of the welcome formulation ;

With great interest I read your advertisement in ....

The requirement profile of your ad ... corresponds in

my opinion, with my qualifications.

For unsolicited applications:

Your renowned company prompted me to this job.

Your high-quality products and good reputation of your company have led me to this job.

A dedicated work in their successful business for me would be of great interest.

Worksheet for the positive welcome formulation

Here you can write variations among each other, which appear to them to be useful in terms of the business and the body and their own feelings and convictions.

With great interest I read your advertisement in ....

The requirement profile your ad in ... corresponds, in my opinion, with my qualifications.

Your different sentences:

-

-

-

-

-

Professional qualifications.

The professional qualification can be found in either the display or a job profile from the Internet.

Is described in the requirement profile in the display, what qualifications you need for the job.

In this part you will describe the qualifications of the main task

For example:

Knowledge and experience with time information in the field of IT, research and development.

Sales experience which products and which target groups.

Experience with the cost accounting and its specific species or activities in the balance sheet or payroll accounting. All times are here, if possible, absolutely necessary.

The scope of the description of your professional qualifications should be limited to 3-4 sentences. It should be short concise sentences. Not be run-on sentences or excessive nested sentences. The sentences should contain no more than three or four bullets.

Example:

For three years I have been working in the IT industry, especially in web design, planning, construction and sales. For two years I have particular experience in the complaint handling and customer acquisition. The tools for creating web design are very familiar to me.

Worksheet for the professional qualifications

To find the relevant or taken qualifications, follow these steps:

Browse creative the display for relevant words or terms that calls for the employer.

Consult possible in the areas where you want to be active professionals.

Think about yourself, what qualifications the employer is asking of them.

What qualifications do you have.

Always remember that the employer wants to hear his

qualification.

Even if you have only partly or not.

In the interview you can still find arguments to achieve this qualification. (Intensive preparation is necessary for this).

Your qualifications, creative collect:

-

-

-

-

Worksheet for the professional qualifications, Page 2

What qualifications are required?

What qualifications are critical with me?

What qualifications do I want to select the letter?

Worksheet for professional qualifications Page 3

Here you can write different sentences, which appear to them to be useful with respect to the company, the location and their own feelings and convictions.

-

-

-

-

-

Personal qualifications.

The personal skills, you can either display or refer to a job profile from the Internet for a speculative application.

Is described in the requirement profile in the display, the personal skills you need for the job.

Smart ads, not necessarily write all the qualifications in the display but expect from you that you know what qualifications, they are expected beyond.

Examples of the personal qualifications:

Teamwork

Engagement, engaged

Initiative

Flexibility

Taking responsibility

Standalone

Cooperative

Competent telephone support

Cooperative team player with excellent communication skills

Strong service orientation

Resilient, high load capacity

Diligence and trustworthiness in the functions: accounting, etc .. Checkout

Creativity is only appropriate where it is required by display or in creative occupations. Otherwise, the creativity is not very desirable.

Again and again met me in my internship the sentence:

Thinking you can (leave or other) leave at the door, here is worked!

Loyalty, loyal

Assertiveness

Good appearance

Positive aura

Motivation

Pleasant appearance

Friendly appearance

Conflict resolution skills

Poise

The detailed justify of the personal properties, as recommended in many applications books, I think is totally missed. It complicates the personnel officer or consultant, the speedy processing and quick reading of the letter.

A short statement regarding the recent work carried out or activities is considered positive.

It is also important that those personal qualities in the job interview, even if it has only limited, can be supported by good arguments.

Given further the book: The job interview.

Examples of the personal qualifications

To take initiative, resilience and committed, team-oriented work I'm used to.

My previous activities as required ... initiative, load capacity and dedicated, team-oriented work.

Responsible behavior and goal-oriented, efficient work under high stress I could put in my previous activities as ... proof.

Careful handling and trustworthy and loyal behavior is natural for me.

My previous activities as .... required a high degree of assertiveness, flexibility and competences, cooperative labor.

Worksheet for the personal qualifications

To find the relevant or taken qualifiers, follow these steps:

Creative: Find relevant words to be important for the employer.

Consult possible in the areas where you want to be active professionals.

Think about yourself, what qualifications the employer is asking of them.

What qualifications do you have.

Always remember that the employer wants to hear his qualification. Even if they have only partly or not. In the interview you can still find arguments to achieve this qualification. (Intensive preparation is necessary for this).

Your qualifications, creative collect:

Worksheet for the professional qualifications, Page 2

What qualifications are required?

What qualifications are critical with me?

What qualifications do I want to select the letter?

Worksheet for personal qualifications Page 3

Here you can write different sentences, which appear to them to be useful in terms of the business and the body and their own feelings and convictions.

-

-

-

-

-

Examples of the final sentence:

On an invitation and a conversation with you I am very pleased.

In an interview with you I am very pleased.

Your company and get to know you, I look forward with great interest.

To work committed to their well-known companies and with them, would be of great interest for me.

Worksheet for positive final sentence

Here you can write variations among each other, which appear to them to be useful in terms of the business and the body and their own feelings and convictions.

On an invitation and to meet you I am very pleased.

In an interview with you I am very pleased.

-

-

-

Curriculum Vitae

Never longer than 1 page !!!!!!!!

For creative or artistic area other possibilities for the design of the CV are possible in the one case or another .

With regard to the clarity and in terms of rapid reading is important to select the tabular form

Otherwise, there are only two main possibilities to structure the CV .

Monthly data : 4. 2012 to 8. 2014

Annual data: 2012-2014

Recruitment wants it short !

Under no circumstances : 1.3.2012 until 01.08.2014

The absolute killer : March 1, 2012 to August 1, 2014

This is a joke , but not unheard of :

first March 2012 to August thirty-firs

CV TABULAR FORM (COMMON FORM)

CV Mary James

2000	Born
Place	Atlanta
2006 – 2010	Primary School, Philadelphia
2010 - 2014	High School, Philadelphia
2016	Bachelor, Lincoln College, Denver
2015	Interschip, 6 Weeks, IBM
2014-2015	Power Seminar, Physic
2013- 2014	Schooler Exchange, England
2013 -	Footballplayer, Dallas

Personal Interests

Computer, Sport

CV TABULAR FORM, Monthly

4. 1996   Born

Place   Dallas

4. 2002 – 8.2006 Primary School, Dallas

8. 2010 – 8.2014 Senior High School, Dallas

8. 2016   Bachelor, Lincoln College, Denver

9. 2015 -10.2015 Intership, IBM, Progamming

9. 2014 - 9.2015 Power Seminar, Physics

10. 2013- 4.2014 Schooler Exchange, England

1. 2013 -   Footballplayer, Dallas

Personal Interests

Computer, Sport

THE MOST SUCCESSFUL CV OF THE WORLD

CV TABULAR FORM (COMMON FORM)

Name	James Joyes
1980	Born
Place	Boston
1999	High School
2001	Bachelor, Russel College, Washington
2004	Master of Science, Biological, MIT, Boston
2005-2008	Research, Development, Pfizer, Atlanta
2009-2013	Area Sales Manager, Glaxo,Texas
Since 2015	Vice President Direct Bussiness, Glaxo
Since 2013	Married, one Child

Further education: Teamworking, Conflict Training,

Leadership Training I,II ,II

Please compare the two proposed tabular CVs in terms of clarity .

The second resume with the monthly data is seamless and is recommended however . With this CV you can hide any times . If you have repeated a school year , were unemployed , have broken off an apprenticeship or received poor marks , you can leave out in the CV

with the years without a break can be seen over time

Worksheet

CV

www.ingramcontent.com/pod-product-compliance
Lightning Source LLC
Chambersburg PA
CBHW070721210526
45170CB00021B/1397